Time and Motion Study

What, Why, and How-To

By Jack Greene

ISBN-13:
978-1466339422

ISBN-10:
146633942X

Time and Motion Study What, Why, and How-To
Table of Contents

Preface
Time and Motion Study
What, Why, and How-To

How long does the job take? Arguably, this is the most valuable fact for a business to know. Both direct and indirect labor costs rely on the required time, as do output, capacity, crew sizes, staffing, schedules, product cost, transfer prices, constraints, workload balance, on and on.

Let's also suggest that the answer must be both accurate and objective.

As with other professions, work measurement proficiency is gained through training and experience. This book explains what to do, why it is necessary, and how to do it; not only study techniques themselves, but also management and control actions to implement work measurement. Both practitioners and managers will learn from the guidance contained.

Since it is a good idea to reduce the amount of work required before it is measured, the chapters also contain improvement suggestions.

Thanks for the purchase. Good luck.

Jack Greene
Jackson Productivity Research Inc.
http://jacksonproductivity.com

September 2011.

About the author and his work measurement background

Jack Greene is president of Jackson Productivity Research Inc. He has implemented dozens of productivity improvement, work measurement, cost reduction, expansion, relocation, consolidation and integration projects in the US and internationally for manufacturing companies both large (Fortune 250) and small.

Mr. Greene is a graduate industrial engineer from the University of Tennessee with over 40 years practical experience in industry, in the U. S. and internationally. He started at U. S. Steel, with a stopwatch in his hand, and subsequently headed division or corporate industrial engineering for three Fortune 250 companies; ITT, Abbott Labs, and Bausch & Lomb.

In all of the management positions, he has directed industrial engineering (cost reduction and productivity, work measurement, cost standards, methods) and facility planning (layout, capacity and cost determination to support strategic decisions, justification of projects, subsequent planning and implementation, plant expansion, relocation, consolidation).

His expertise in cost effective manufacturing and management practices comprehends the semiconductor, pharmaceutical, optical, steel, lighting, electronic assembly, canning, recreational, consumer products, and hospitality and communication industries. He has frequently represented manufacturing and facility interests within due diligence and feasibility studies for merger, acquisition and consolidation projects.

Emphasizing individual, boutique attention, JPR can also provide scalable, comprehensive, on-site project management through its network of well qualified domestic and international affiliates.

Other books on Amazon address management and how-to techniques for:

Cost Reduction   How to Survive, Recover, Thrive
Plant Design, Plant Layout, Floor Planning
Facility Relocation, Expansion, Consolidation, Site Search

Chapter 1.
Benefits of work measurement, perhaps the most important management tool

How long does the job take? Arguably, this is the most valuable fact for a business to know. Possess this simple bit of information and your organization can:

- quantify the amount of labor you'll pay for
- determine staffing levels as output levels vary
- calculate actual capacity the operation can produce
- assign and schedule work to people and equipment
- identify lost time, waste, non-value added activity
- offer pay related to output, labor incentives
- define the cost for the products and services you offer
- balance lines or work groups for optimum performance
- analyze variance to find problems
- identify and manage constraints, equipment, process, facility
- justify equipment and automation acquisition
- meet the Sarbanes Oxley Act for financial understanding of costs
- compare the cost to install and service products in the field, yours and competitors

This how-to book provides the detail to measure work, as well as to administer a measurement program accurately and fairly.

Work measurement is just as effective in the office, the lab, the maintenance shop, the field, the customer service unit, and the warehouse as it is on a production floor.

◆ ◆ ◆

Set expectations, measure and communicate

You, and I, and the people in your company want to know what is expected of them (and their group and the company) and how well they do against expectations. Measure work and see how well you produce results.

In this economy, people are more apprehensive than usual, so expectations and measurement and communication are even more important.

One of my good bosses, and I have been blessed to have several, gave out wall plaques that said Results Count. Work measurement can be measured, and results can be quantified and compared.

One of my good clients, and I have been blessed to have several, asked me to set up an incentive system for his construction supervisors. And we did; but he really wanted, first, to establish a reporting system of work done, blocks laid and slabs poured and time lost, as a visible record that highlighted problems and usually solutions. That system to express expectations and measure performance was a key part of the improvement that followed.

Generally when "Productivity" is discussed, we really mean "Labor", the people side of the manufacturing enterprise. That cost will not usually be the largest, but because labor produces the organization's services and products, its performance is critical beyond the mere cost.

Just because there are complicating factors to work measurement, do not stop the effort to measure. Recognize that answers may not be perfectly accurate, but still perform useful service. And you can fine tune the initial mechanism to yield ever better results.

◆　◆　◆

Caveat

Be advised that the results of any measurement can report only part of the story, the final result; it does not report what caused the result. For instance, the much emulated Toyota Production System emphasizes personal development of line workers and supervisors, which is usually accomplished by training. In a work measurement result, training will appear to be unproductive time but would shortly lead to even higher productivity as learned lessons are put into effect.

Chapter 2.
Which measurement technique?
Choose to fit your objectives, budget, timetable

A. Choose an approach to fit your objectives, budget, timetable.
There are many circumstances for which work measurement is an attractive strategy. A technique will address different objectives, budgets, and timetables differently.

You may choose from a limited scope of work measurement, or a vast undertaking; set narrow objectives or the establishment of work measurement as the basis for an integrated approach to control. Put forth an initial phase, accomplish it and review costs and benefits, then take the next step.

None of the strategies is inherently useful, by the way. You may have the right reasons but select the wrong methodology and eventually be dissatisfied.

◆ ◆ ◆

B. Do you want to set incentives or quantify expectations or balance workload?
Your purpose will influence the type of measurement.

Four types of systems generally cover most work measurement.
Measured day work does not involve a difference in pay for different output. Labor standards, or rates, are developed in an organized fashion, but perhaps with less attention to detail than incentives. Typically the supervisor or manager will administer a control method, by which the output of each operator is recorded daily and compared to a norm.

Reasonable expectancies are an engineered standard, perhaps with less measurement and less definition of methods and interference. Often the jobs are less structured and more variable so that close documentation is not cost justified. Typically the supervisor or manager will administer a control method, by which the output of each operator is recorded daily and compared to expectancies.

Engineered standards is the term for data which have been objectively and rationally collected for the purpose of definition and control of operations. It can include labor, equipment and capacity expectations and standard cost information.

Incentives, piece work are systems to pay for output. More output that meets quality specs, more pay. Incentives will usually be carefully developed as regards the one best way, pace rating during observation, and number of observations of several operators. Incentives require a level of administrative support as well, because each operator's performance must be calculated daily and pay rates administered.

Generally, incentives are more carefully developed than measured day work, which is more carefully developed than reasonable expectancies.

A difference in opinion about workload may arise in any of the categories, and is usually addresses by targeted time study of relatively short duration. It is a "quick fix" as opposed to the four longer term programs.

◆ ◆ ◆

C. What is the appropriate tool; time study, work sample or predetermined times?
First let's describe them.

1. Observation time study
The original idea was to observe work, time how long it took and write it down. Although there are now better equipment and technical nuances, that is still the idea.

The elements of work on a production floor usually repeat, often quite rapidly. Work elements in an office, a lab, a maintenance facility, a construction unit may not repeat as frequently. In both cases the work can be observed and recorded, but not necessarily with the same watch or observation sheet.

In order to observe and quantify work times, a standard stop watch with a sweep hand has been the norm, but digital readouts with big numbers are easier to read and PDA or iPhone apps are available. A video camera can be used, in order to create a permanent record or allow discussion later. Reading the tape takes no less time in the office, and an observer on the floor provides much more flexibility to ask questions or make mid-course correction during the study.

Look at the particular job you will observe and set up an observation sheet beforehand based on the elements in a repetitive cycle. Then start observing, record the elements in a cycle, then repeat as the operator does.

For measurement of a job which does not repeat frequently, the observation sheet may be blank to start because you will be taking a lot of notes to explain the times you see. Any watch that you can read easily will do, again digital is better.

You will have to keep one eye on the work, one on the watch, one on the observation sheet. If an element creates a sound when it happens, use that to help you pick up the work time. Write what you see on the watch, don't round. Electronic devices help those without three eyes.

Work measurement may be of an operator, a machine, a process, a movement, any element of work whose duration is important. Don't assume that a mechanism will always take the same amount of time to perform its function; that is not always true.

Fast moving technology may be alleviating the time study burden. Several software products have been on the market for years, designed to operate PDA's. The programs are written to allow the user to perform work measurement by pushing the keys in a predetermined manner. They used the PDA to enter observations of the work, and connected to computer spread sheets for summary and analysis.

Great idea. They reduce the engineering time in several ways and improve accuracy, especially for repetitive studies. Set up the study in advance, then keep your eye on the work while you push keys to record times.

As in many other endeavors, Apple has introduced a new paradigm. There are now iPhone based time study apps for a few dollars, that appear to be quite appropriate; with full featured programs, downloadable to computer, although I haven't tried one. Apps for Android phones are appearing; decide whether you want to have the entire system on your own phone and computer, or whether you want a hosted program for analysis and archiving, on a subscription basis.

JPR does not have a relationship with any of these companies, but likes the concept and what I have seen of the mechanisms to perform the actual work measurement and later to summarize the study and accumulate results into standard Excel format. Search and see what is available; technology moves quickly.

2. Work sample, random sample, or the old term ratio delay. Originally "ratio delay" determined the amount of work, and of delay, through work observation at random times, not continually. Work sample is a more modern phrase, but measures the same way, not continually but randomly. Work sampling is a most effective way to learn quickly about an unfamiliar situation with several interdependent activities. It can even be used to understand general aspects of repetitive functions where many people perform the same work. And of course it quantifies delay and non-cyclic activity quite well.

Please note that continuous time study is also a work sample; it is just all at once whereas random sampling is spread out over a longer time. There is little difference in philosophy, just in logistics.

In practice, work sampling may be done in person or with video recording. One operation may be observed, or multiple operations and people, allied or dissimilar.

Select random times for the observer to start rounds, in order to see all conditions throughout a time frame, because some work occurs differently at startup, or shift change. Some work occurs during steady state operation and some at changeover. An observer may also stay in the area constantly, finish a round then start another.

The observer must prepare in advance by recording all of the equipment and people to be observed, and all of the categories of activity and non-activity to be recorded.

If the study objective is to quantify "delay", or "work" in total for a group, then accurate results will be quickly evident. If the objective is to differentiate between different work elements, and different causes for delay during different times of day then the observation sheet will be more complicated and accurate results will take longer (but probably be more useful).

Personally I prefer work sampling of multiple operations more or less continually to learn generally what goes on in a work center. I would record work, delay and interference instances fairly definitively, while asking questions; what and why. I'll see how work is assigned and followed, what other people interrelate. Quantify times and frequencies. Later, zero in on the specific work with time study.

3. Pre-determined times
Predetermined times are proprietary systems that have over long observation developed the amount of time required for basic motions. The Gilbreth's started the concept with "Therbligs", 17 basic motions and their times.

As the name implies, pre-determined systems have been developed in advance, and a particular motion is defined to require a certain time. Motions groups have been combined into tasks, to reduce the time to apply the rates, to build up useful values.

Modern proprietary pre-determined systems include MTM, Modapts, MSD. MOST, Work Factor, and adaptations developed by companies such as Siemens.

Practitioners have their preferences, as each vendor will be considered to be superior for one or another application, such as a factory, or office, or warehouse.

Work factor and MTM, Methods-Time Measurement, recognize extremely short motions that occur in highly repetitive motions. These motions don't take long in the first place, and because of very frequent repetition and muscle memory, operators require even less time than perhaps the book allows. Such "ballistic" motions are not uncommon in repetitive work, and if you will measure them you had better use a detailed system such as MTM.

Modapts, MSD and MOST, accumulate predetermined times into larger groups. For highly repetitive work they may not be as accurate as MTM but for more variable work they can take significantly less time to apply.

Warehouse and distribution centers practitioners have their favorites as well, swearing by particular programs.

In any of these proprietary systems you must deal with one of the sponsoring organizations, and become accredited in application. Please see the web sites for the particular organizations.

The author is not accredited in pre-determined times, but calls on experts when necessary.

◆ ◆ ◆

D. Options for work measurement; choose to fit your objectives
An organization has a choice of techniques. This section will discuss options, to relate the objective to the most appropriate techniques. Work measurement assists an organization to improve productivity, but let's get more specific. "Productivity" is a worthwhile goal, but organizations usually face a more well defined challenge. Just exactly what action does one take, in a particular situation?

1. Resolve short term issues
   ◆ Arbitrate a disagreement about workload; is a particular position or crew overloaded, or underloaded. Employ a short, objective, focused time study or work sampling; few days or a week.

♦ Clear up bottlenecks which constrain production. Scope will depend on number of bottlenecks. Identify the bottleneck thru performance records or local knowledge. Observe, use time study, work sampling, man-machine charts to quantify. Manage constraint by rearranging work elements, relieve, change speeds, accumulation, consider equipment acquisition.

♦ Balance workloads so that crew members have approximately the same amount of work. Use time study and work sampling to quantify activity; rearrange work elements or flow; consider equipment acquisition.

♦ Routinely monitor crew workloads, that they are within expectations, perhaps to prepare for union negotiations. Apply work sampling, with a single set of written guidelines, for uniform and consistent results.

2. Options to establish an extensive work measurement system.
In all cases, build a data bank of the information collected, to standardize the rates set and reduce application cost.

♦ Short cycle jobs, for incentive.   Predetermined times, MTM or Work factor

♦ Longer cycle, for incentive. Predetermined times, Modapts, MOST, MSD. Confirm with work sample.

♦ Longer cycle, reasonable expectancies.   Modapts, MOST, MSD, time study, work sample.

♦ Standard cost.   Observe actual situation; time study, work sample.

◆ Indirect manpower. Understand where indirect manpower spends time, in order to allocate overhead accurately; apply work sample.

3. Further detail about the attributes of Time Study and Work Sampling

There are several factors to consider in order to select time study or sampling. Often both time study and work sampling should be used, each will be useful for one purpose and less useful for another.

a. Purpose of work measurement
What is the purpose of the measurement? If you want to set an incentive standard for assemblers seated at a workbench, time study (or predetermined times) is the choice. If your objective is to determine an approximate workload of material handlers, maintenance, or inspectors spread across a warehouse, sampling is a good choice.

Work sampling is a most effective way to learn quickly about an unfamiliar situation with several interdependent activities. It can even be used to understand general aspects of repetitive functions where many people perform the same work. And of course it quantifies delay and non-cyclic activity quite well.

Two sections below have a significant effect on the choice of measurement technique as well, practice opportunity and crew size.

b. Objectives and mechanics of observations
1) Time study is continual observation, in order to record all the activity that a person performs over a period of time. The observer

will define and time all activity, work, delay, personal, interruptions, problems, whatever, for the person observed. Usually the observation period is over a short period of time, often for 50 cycles, or 100 cycles of operator performance. Observation may be repeated later for other workers.

2) Work sampling is periodic observation repeated over a longer time; a record of what activity occurs at the particular instant of time when the observer is looking at the activity. Usually intermittent times are selected at random, many observations repeated over a time frame, so that the observer does not appear in the area on a predictable pattern or path. Several people can easily be observed during one study, a crew or work group. I like to walk into the work area, and when I am in a position to see all the activity, observe many workers at a glance, then stop to record what I have seen.

c. Statistics
Both time study and sampling are statistical processes. The accuracy of the resulting work measurement is a function of the number of observations, and there are statistical formulae of accuracy versus observations.

One factor that generates accuracy rapidly for sampling is crew size; one sample is at a given time, but you will observe all of the people in a crew.

d. Practice opportunity
1. Time study will be more effective to measure workers who repeat the same motions very frequently, with short cycle times. Higher practice opportunity will allow these people to have highly repetitive motions and little variation from the allowed time.

2. Sampling is best for people who have a wider range of work elements and longer cycle times. They may well perform the same

actions repetitively, but with less frequency, therefore will have less opportunity to develop highly repetitive motions. In this category are material handlers, shipping and receiving, maintenance both demand and preventive, tenders of automatic machines, inspectors, set up and changeover, cleanup workers, installers, field workers, customer service, any troubleshooting.

e. Crew size
1. A time study can record well what one person does and how long it takes. It is even possible to view two or maybe three at the same time, but it takes skill.

2. Sampling works very well as a measure of a crew or work group, even if spread over a geographic area such as a plant or warehouse floor. If their work is related, so much the better because the observation sheet can record when two more are working together, as well as how the available work is spread out at each observation. An observer may not record the activity of all the crew at the same instant; that is not a problem but be sure to account for all members each cycle.

f. Delay and random occurrence; as necessary elements
The old name of work sampling was "ratio delay", for it was used effectively to determine the amount of delay in a process, over a period of time. That is still an excellent reason to use sampling, especially if several interrelated people of machines are involved. The downside is that many observations are necessary to accumulate an accurate evaluation for one individual machine, or process, or person.

Time study is usually for a relatively short time, while sampling observations usually take place over a longer period of time. As a result of a longer cycle, sampling has a better statistical chance of seeing very infrequent random elements of work or delay, and may even pick up observations for bench workers who have been time studied.

4. Results standardization through pre-determined times

The US Department of Defense is requiring suppliers in some instances to justify the costs of their products. As a result, my friends tell me, pre-determined times are usually the choice to measure the work of building a helicopter, or bomber. Pre-determined times are a good choice for this measurement because they are designed to state times for the same task consistently and repeatably. The pre-determined time companies require certification of practitioners, to maintain a level of proficiency.

Traditionally, pre-determined times are said to be an additive process, and time study a subtractive process. A pre-determined rate is established by defining the work and assigning a time value; the elements can be added up in an office without seeing the process. A time study takes place at the work station, the watch runs, and the rate will be what the watch says, minus whatever the observer deems unnecessary. While this characterization is not flattering to either system, is is essentially true.

In either case, when an organization administers the process fairly and intelligently, good results may be expected. The converse is also true.

◆ ◆ ◆

Chapter 3
The art of the time study

A. Work measurement purposes
The purpose of work measurement is to determine as objectively as possible the time required for particular tasks, then to convert those times into an work expectation that is possible and practical, all day, day after day.

A qualified work measurement practitioner can do that with only a timing device, good judgment about what constitutes work, a set of policies from management, and a calculator.

The sequence of events is simple: observe the work and record the time an "operator" takes to complete it; "pace rate" the observed work; add "allowances" for fatigue, break, lunch; convert to "units" per hour or day. All of those events are objective except for one, pace rating.

Time study, time and motion study are just as effective in the office, the lab, the maintenance shop, the field, customer service, and the warehouse as on a production floor. Just about anywhere your organization had a presence.

◆ ◆ ◆

B. Axioms
When you take a "time study",
1. Let everyone concerned know that you are making a study. When asked, answer questions about your purpose, objectives and technique as accurately as possible.

2. Stand up, never sit during the observations. Even when the operator is sitting.

3. Position yourself near the person or persons being studied, so you can observe the action.

4. Understand the actions being performed, and their "sequence".

5. If there is something you don't understand, ask. Do not assume. But don't ask questions while the "clock" is running.

6. If the study is "continuous", take breaks and lunch when the one you study does.

7. Act professionally while in the workplace. Use appropriate safety equipment.

8. Study only trained, experienced "operators". Study more than one operator if possible, on different shifts.

9. Observe only operators who use the accepted "best method" in order to establish a "rate". If your purpose is to identify and quantify the method differences, view all the candidates.

◆ ◆ ◆

C. Company policy will affect work measurement

1. Standard method
Is an employee required to perform a task one particular way, or allowed to ad lib? In some industries, pharmaceuticals for instance, there is only one way. Period. A non-standard method may lead to a fatal problem.

How about making thumbtacks, or ad spots, or sales calls? Uniformity is valuable there too, for practical or financial rather than life threatening reasons.

Your organization may have invested to develop a process that will produce the greatest efficiency, or success rate, or quality level, or customer service, or acceptance. You will ask a trainee to use the method that produces best results. Your organization may call the best method by any name, but be sure that it is followed.

2. Expected performance, whether of production or office or service or construction workers.
Presumably your organization is interested in work measurement in order to quantify expected performance. These points will help explain expected performance.

Employees are expected to perform, in exchange for pay. This is true of people on an assembly line, farmers, sales clerks, bricklayers, stockbrokers, service technicians, a CEO, of me and of you. Performance is sometimes called a fair day's work for a fair day's pay.

An expectation can be defined, "that which an average trained, qualified operator will produce over a certain time period, working at good speed and effort."

Expected performance must include all of the factors which are required, specifically including the time to perform the cyclic work elements, "as necessary" tasks such as aside the last and get the next material; setup, cleanup, break, lunch.

Expected performance is that work which is within the control of the operator; the operator generally does not control material flow and should not be held responsible for lack of material or the time lost waiting for it. The same theory holds true for quality of incoming material and of equipment delay; management must not hold an operator responsible for that.

◆ ◆ ◆

D. Preparation for time study

Note that there is no inherently right or wrong technique in the following sections; each can have a place where it is superior to others. Some techniques will fit your application, while others will be unlikely to achieve the accuracy and cost objectives.

1. What comes first, methods or work measurement?

This is a chicken-and-the-egg question which implies a linear relationship. In fact, methods and work measurement are a circular progression; perform one then the other alternately over time. If you start with methods improvement, quickly you will want to evaluate methods and you will have to time them to compare. Start with measurement, quickly you will identify other methods and will have to choose one. When Frederick Taylor wrote the book on work measurement in the late 1800's, one of his first revelations was the relationship between methods and the time to perform them. As you write your own studies, you will confirm the relationship.

The only bad choice is to fail to start somewhere.

Taylor invented the concept of "The one best way" and the Gilbreth's emphasized it as well. Their objective is to find the one best way, and require that operators follow that way. In these less rigorous times, a tendency may be to allow leeway in an operator's motion pattern. But one standard method is required in the pharmaceutical industry, and electronics, where an operator's ad lib can literally be a matter of life or death. A company is better off with "The one best way" for all the right reasons.

Ergonomics is not the topic of this document but a special note is worthwhile. Ergonomic work design is usually cost justified because if there is less stress there will be less cost, in both the short run and the long term. Avail yourself with current ideas about ergonomic work design and build the principles into your methods development; you and your employees will be grateful.

2. How many observations are necessary?

Work measurement is a statistical process. Your objective is to sample a work process and learn information about it that you can use for management purposes. Both work sample and time study use statistics; time study in a concentrated manner for a short period of time and sampling less frequently over a longer period.

Statistical sampling is effective when there is a homogeneous universe at work; typically represented by a normal or bell curve. Even if a normal curve exists in your situation, there will be times of the day when circumstances are different. In any job, there will be start up conditions, shut down, clean up, steady state. There will be times when materials are not available on a constant basis, or are of variable quality. There will be new products, regular products, spec changes, machine problems.

Observe during situations when conditions are "normal" because your objective is to sample average conditions. Also observe early and late, before and after shift change, break, lunch.
Observe enough cycles to assure that a representative cross section of the work is seen and recorded. There is statistical information available to help to determine the correct number of observations, but the use of the rates developed affects the statistics as well. If you intend to establish incentive standards, you will need to make more observations than if you intend only a general understanding of relative activity. But in either case, if you will establish expectations of people and set crew sizes and workloads, you had better be on a firm foundation because there will be a reaction from the people involved.

In August 2011 there was a thoroughly constructive discussion on Linked In, Work Measurement and Engineered Standards group, many knowledgeable people sharing what they know well. The question was "how many studies are necessary to take, in order to set a correct standard?" The questioner knew that there are statistical methods, formulae, and tables to calculate a number but was interested in "rules of thumb."

The following will list the suggestions, along with my own thoughts, that appear to be the most practical, but non-statistical ideas.

- Do not study an operator who is not trained, with some experience. Period. Don't do it.

- The flip side of inexperience is to look around for an operator who has obviously superior talent or skill. You will recognize it when you see it. It may not be possible for all operators to gain the skill, but there may be opportunity to define superior methods or motion patterns for others to use.

- The first question is," What are the standards to be used for?" Typical choices are measured day work, reasonable expectancies, engineered standards, a formal incentive program, which are explored elsewhere. They are progressively more stringent, requiring progressively more time study work and rigor, which includes more studies. Incentives require the most because both employee pay and company incentive bonus will be affected.

- Another early factor is element length and practice opportunity. Shorter work elements allow more practice opportunity and faster learning, so that an operator will soon develop "ballistic" motion patterns that don't vary much for one operator. Study multiple trained operators, and for short cycle tasks their observed times will repeat closely.

- If not, find the best operator and retrain others.

- Team standards may be more difficult to study, to define closely, and to summarize if multiple possibilities for task assignment and sequence are possible. Find the best ways first, and study them. Concentrate here, as in all tasks, on the critical path, the constraint, the limiting activity.

- Record the observed times for the studies, and for short cycle tasks you will probably find they quickly fall in a narrow range, and the cumulative average is steady. Five percent is usually considered a reasonable variation. That's enough study. Move on.

- A corollary is that longer cycle jobs have less opportunity repetition, and thus longer learning and more observed variation. You may require more observations to reach a point with little statistical variation. But these elements many each be only a small part of the total work process, so that variation will have less impact on the overall time study rate.

- If your purpose is to find a superior motion pattern by the way, you will want to break the job down into small elements in order to zero in on differences.

- Shorter studies seem to be favored over long ones, with constant summary and comparison of results. When the cumulative data don't change much, you have enough.

- Be sure to observe different operators on different shifts to cover all operating conditions.

♦ Be alert to different operating conditions at different times of the day; especially for non-cyclic elements caused by outside influences; instructions, questions, deliveries, shipments, procedures. Consider a production study, a long continuous study of one operator, to uncover infrequent non-cyclic occurrences and interruptions. Correct the reasons for interruption, rather than including them in the rate.

♦ If the job has a fixed machine content, that doesn't need to be studied as much. However, in a man-machine cycle, you may have nothing to do in that period, but to time.

♦ Once the standard is set, especially if it covers many people or important steps, validate it with an additional study.
♦ Can product mix affect the answer? What about fatigue because of weight, heat, awkward working positions, or 12 hour shift?

3. Individual variation

It is very educational to observe a really qualified operator. If you have seen other people first, you may have thought that you understood the job. A really good operator will work with a smoothness that less qualified do not have, good speed but not necessarily a killer pace. No missteps, no unnecessary motions. The better operators may also have a superior motion pattern, and if so you will want to teach it to others.

Better operators also have better quality. Check it out. Speed does not necessarily cause defects. Fast operators tend to repeat their motion patterns very closely, often "ballistic" motions, and the repetition reduces mistakes.

Motivated operators, for instance those on a pay incentive, will exceed those who are not on incentive. The best operator I ever saw, over many years, was that combination of a really qualified operator, at a short cycle job, on incentive and wanting to earn, with exemplary quality. The company incentive plan paid for more output; both employee and employer achieved their goals.

4. Units of measure

Choose the units of measure carefully. Some will be clear; if the operator assembles a complete product, or subassembly, the unit of measure will be the product or subassembly. If a crew lays a brick wall, the units will be brick laid, hundreds or thousands. If a similar crew pours a concrete slab, the unit will be slabs, one.

The other measure than output will be of input, usually man hours. The unit of input could as easily be man-seconds, or man-minutes, but man hours per unit (or per hundred or thousand), is easier to calculate and perform the arithmetic for.

5. Element length

Elements have to be long enough so that you can observe them, read the watch, and record the time before the next reading is due. The advantage to selecting a shorter element is that variations will be easier to identify. Shorter elements will usually lead to a more accurate standard, but require more work on the part of the observer and in the office, to total and average data. Shorter elements are more necessary for tasks of a short cycle, less necessary for longer cycle tasks.

6. Individual or crew standards

Usually it will be clear whether to develop and apply individual or crew measurement. As a general rule, individual rates are more accurate but require more work both to develop and to administer. If teamwork is really required, crew rates will probably be more satisfactory, although there may be complaints in either case that some people do not carry their fair load.

7. Sequence

Plan the study after understanding the sequence. Determine the composition of the "elements" that you will record; they should be natural steps in the total cycle. It will help your study if there is a definite sound at the end of the element, so that you will be sure that the element is complete even if you don't see it. Otherwise use a specific, clearly defined motion with a change of motion at the end of the element. For instance, a put-away is a good end point of a cycle, with the first element of the next cycle to obtain the next part and move it to the work area. Subsequent elements could be steps in the overall cycle.

The element must be long enough for you to have time to read the watch and record the time. Otherwise, shorter cycles tend to define the work more accurately.

8. Before the study, record the elements on the "time study form" that you will fill out during the observation; because during the study you will have little time to write.

♦ ♦ ♦

E. The study technique, while on the job

1. Observe the operator actions for a few "cycles" in order to understand the sequence of events and your own technique.

There are two kinds of stopwatch studies, "continuous" and "snapback".

If you use snapback, you must use a two or three watch board, set up stop one watch while snapping back and starting another. An advantage is that the observer can read a stopped watch hand instead of a moving one. Another advantage is that the observer will record the value which is the observed time. Refer to http://www.meylan.com/tsboards.html. Meylan is a fine name in timestudy and will provide high quality equipment. And I don't get a commission.

Continuous timestudy uses one watch that is not reset. An advantage is that all time is accounted for; a disadvantage is that recorded times must be subtracted in the office later to get the observed time.

Snapback takes no time to subtract in the office, but with continuous you will have a better audit trail in case of unexpected variation during the study; the watch continues to run as an accurate record. Generally if there is little variation in the work patterns, such as an individual short cycle job with consistent conditions, snapback will be very effective and accurate. If there is likely to be variation in sequence, or elements are long, or the unexpected may occur, or teamwork is involved then continuous study is preferred.

2. During observation, you will want to keep one eye on the watch and one eye on the operator. And one eye on the form where you enter the "reading". This will take some practice for you to gain proficiency.

3. Read the watch to the second, or hundredth, but do not round off to the nearest 5 for instance.

4. Record the reading immediately to the time study form. Make and record a pace rating.

5. You may choose to record times with a pencil or a pen. If a pencil, the readings will tend to smudge and be indistinct. If a pen, you will make errors and have to cross out the entry. My preference is the pen, so that any error correction is part of the record, and entries are easy to read.

6. If there is an obvious problem; an operator drops a tool or part, or a machine malfunctions, "red circle" it; call attention to the instance on the form and explain it with a note. Later, determine if the situation should be allowed or not in the rate.

7. Pace rating
Recently a reader of my web site asked, "If Mr. Average can achieve 100%, then a faster person can achieve 120% or even 140%. I seek your advice whether there is a simple website where I can read this industrial standards."

My answer. thanks for the inquiry. I believe there is not a simple answer for your question, but I will explain some of basic ideas, and provide some references.

Yes, average is considered to be 100%.

Yes, some people can perform at higher levels of output.

Yes, there is a website for modern pace rating CD's. Bob McClure offers guidance at www.rbtmcclureassoc.com.

Now, some discussion
a. "Performance" is composed of several factors.
One is effort, how hard a person works.

Two is skill, because a skillful person will produce more at less effort than a hard working beginner.

Three is methods. Correct methods must be determined first, and the people trained.

Fourth is practice opportunity, or learning curve. Learning curve applies to individuals because a person never stops improving; the rate of improvement will decrease but not stop. The practical aspect of learning curve is that hand motions will become more and more smooth, and will repeat without conscious thought, through muscle memory. Motions become "ballistic", arced, rather than straight lines and turns.

Five is <u>motivation</u>. Even skillful trained workers can often increase performance when motivated through pay, pride, challenge, or other physical or emotional urge.

Six, and an ingredient of all, is <u>quality</u>. In my experience the most skillful operators are the ones with the highest quality. I reject the opinion that speed automatically causes a drop in quality. It may do so, but not with a skillful operator.

b. High task, low task
Many believe that there are two tiers of performance, high task and low task, Low task is considered to define jobs which are not carefully measured, do not have an incentive pay rate, are relatively long cycle jobs without being completely repetitive.

High task jobs would be on incentive, short cycle, carefully measured, highly repetitive.

You might see 120% performance against a high or low task job, but if standards are well set a higher performance should be uncommon. If you set a low task standard then start paying an incentive rate for the job, performance could easily be 140%.

c. Pace rating on the job
A skillful industrial engineer will be able to observe an operator during time study and apply pace rating. The engineer will use a watch to record times, then multiply the observation by pace rating to create what is called "allowed time" for a task. Allowed time is the time required for an average (but trained) operator working at average skill and effort to perform a given task. If an operator

takes ten second to do an element and is rated at 120%, the allowed time is 12 seconds.

Personally I find that different portions of a job may be done with different skill and effort so I apply a pace rating to each job element.

8. Cyclical and non-cyclical elements

Elements which are performed for each cycle are easy to observe and account for. "As necessary", or non-cyclic, elements are those which are necessary to keep an operation going. They typically include acts such as aside a full container of finished parts, get a new container of parts to assemble, refill a supply container, fill out a required document, receive instructions, workplace maintenance that the operator is responsible for. Necessary but non-cyclical work may include set up, put away, clean, talk to supervisor; they must be observed and built into a standard at the frequency with which they occur.

Pace rating must be observed independent of the cyclical elements. Non-cyclical elements should not include delay; do not include wait for materials, or outside maintenance.

9. You will find that you reduce the possibility of error or misunderstanding when you read the watch and record times fairly often during a non-repetitive study. You as the observer will not always know what is to be done next, and there will be occurrences when you do not understand the action, or lack of it. Eventually, you will ask or sort out the action, but some period of elapsed time will be poorly defined. Probably you will want to disregard, toss out, the poorly defined time. If you have recorded time frequently, the length of the poorly defined sequence will be minimized.

10. Activity of people as they interact with machines is often a factor in many jobs. People can load and unload machines, or load and someone elsewhere unloads; people may activate and wait; they may tend a nominally automatic machine. Interaction with a keyboard or computer is quite common.

A classic distinction relates to waiting; does the machine wait on the person or does the person wait on the machine? The terms Internal and External are used; an "internal" element is performed by a person while the machine is performing its function. An "external" element is done by a person while the machine waits.

Which is the bottleneck, or constraint? Usually the objective will be to keep the bottleneck in operation, don't let it wait.

A good visual tool is called a "man - machine chart". First it is necessary to time the work of the people and of the machine. The man - machine chart then is simply a plot of the times, to represent what happens and when. Specifically it is useful to determine how to reduce the cycle of the bottleneck.

Be aware that machine speeds are not necessarily fixed, they often may be sped up or slowed down. There is probably an optimum speed that will yield the most effective performance considering machine and operator wait times, product quality, machine reliability and maintenance.

11. As you time a crew operation, with one watch running, you may want to record multiple elemental times; to note the time when a particular sub-task is complete, or milestone completed. Such added detail will increase your understanding of time required and of crew interaction.

12. Lost. Someday the operator you are observing will lose you, by stepping through a door or up a stair or into an elevator. It will

happen. Smile it off, and go on about your business.

♦ ♦ ♦

E. Summary after the study
1. Arithmetic in general
The practitioner observes work, reads a watch, and writes down on the time study form that time, called the observed time. The practitioner also writes down a pace rating. Later in the office, the observed time is multiplied by the pace rating and the result is the normal time.

All normal times for a particular element, or task, are averaged for all operators who are observed. Allowances are then added to the average normal time, and the result is called the standard time. A very satisfactory unit is hours per thousand pieces; this works well in financial calculations. The reciprocal is pieces per hour, which is good information for workers to know what is expected of them.

2. Each study
Treat each study as an entity; do all the arithmetic and summarize findings.
Subtract if you have a continuous study, to find all of the individual observed times. Multiply them by the pace rating factor. Total, divide by number of observations and average. Enter all of the data for the study, description, total reading, number of observations, and average. Summarize any notes made. Determine the disposition of any "red circled" data.

3. Running summary
Start a running summary for each job, or set of data. Enter each study into the running summary, and calculate the results of all data to date. Determine when there is enough data to yield the statistical accuracy. Judge when other operators, other shifts, should be studied.

When data are sufficient, write out the complete operation, and apply allowances.

4. Allowances

Allowances are a part of standards in order to account for employee break and lunch and trips to the rest room. There is also often a consideration for fatigue, and for factors that appear in some jobs such as high heat loads and heavy weights. These factors may be a legal requirement, or a part of contractual negotiations, or part of management policy.

Allowances may or may not be built into a standard depending on how it is to be applied. You will find, experience tells me, that measurement is easier to administer arithmetically if you build allowances in. First quantify the work time, perhaps 8 or 8.5 or 12 hours. Then convert the allowances to hours, and subtract from the nominal work shift. For instance, with a 8.5 hour shift, subtract .5 hours for lunch; .5 hours for two 15 minute work and rest room breaks; .1 hour end-of-shift clean up; .2 hours equivalent for fatigue. Subtract 1.3 hours from 8.5; operators are expected to be on the job and working 7.2 hours per shift. Divide 8.5 by 7.2, and the allowance factor is 1.18. Multiply this factor by the average normal time.

5. Calculate the rate
   ♦ Determine the standard time and the rate required.
   ♦ Add in factors for relief, lunch, breaks, rest rooms per company policy. The arithmetic can be done several ways, applying factors over the shift, over (the shift minus factors), considering paid or unpaid lunch, contracts, etc.
   ♦ Prepare a set of operator instructions for the job as studied.
   ♦ Publish rate and instructions. Enter the new rate into whichever management tools are fed by the standards.

6. Standard data

Standard data is a formal collection of information about your particular operation. Standard data is simply a library, the data base that you have accumulated. Standard data should be a part of your work measurement tool kit, especially because it is so easy in the computer age.

Work measurement data may be obtained, organized and collated from any source; for instance from predetermined times or time study observations of similar operations.

After the library has enough data to be accurate, apply standard data to determine the time to perform future work in instances with similar circumstances, so that rates are consistent. Using standard data probably will take less work to set future rates, but data maintenance is required to assure it is accurate. For a new rate, you will need to define the work conditions by direct observation so that proper time values can be selected that match the work being done.

When you time operations and develop time values, name and define them carefully and file. Then go into your library in the future, to build a new rate that includes a previously recorded elemental time, or a standard time.

When you collect values, list not only the time but also the number of observations, and the date and circumstances. Later, compare and add new values especially to increase the number of observations and therefore the accuracy of the data.

♦ ♦ ♦

Chapter 4
The art of work sampling

Work Sampling Primer

Work sampling is one tool that can be useful to measure work through observation and note-taking. Work sampling is a most effective way to learn quickly about a situation with several interdependent activities, perhaps a department or section. It can even be used to understand general aspects of repetitive functions where many people perform the same work. And of course it quantifies delay and non-cyclic activity quite well.

Please note that continuous time study is also a work sample; it is just all at once whereas random sampling is spread out over a longer time. There is little difference in philosophy, just in logistics.

A. Work sample, or random sample; the old term was ratio delay. Originally "ratio delay" determined the amount of work, and of delay, through work observation at random times, not continually. Work sample is a more modern phrase, but measures the same way, not continually but randomly. Work sample can be used widely, to observe and generate information about any actual activities of people, or equipment, or processes.

In practice, work sampling may be done in person or with video recording. One operation may be observed, or multiple operations and people, allied or dissimilar.

Personally I prefer work sampling of multiple operations more or less continually to learn generally what goes on in a work center. I would record work, delay and interference instances fairly definitively, while asking questions; what and why. See how work is assigned and followed, what other people interrelate.

An effective practice is to quantify a wide variety of activities and their and frequencies with work sampling. Later, if you need to learn more detail, zero in on the most important specific work with time study.

◆ ◆ ◆

B. Observer bias

An observer can introduce bias into a study. Consciously or unconsciously an observer may expect to see a particular activity by an individual. An observer may develop a feeling for a certain individual based on early observations and project that feeling into later rounds.

Be careful to prevent any bias; write down what you see. Do not try to prove a point by a study. An outside observer, a consultant, will be more likely to report honestly and fairly. In many cases time study or work sampling will be used to resolve objectively a union - management disagreement; I have been called in for that purpose, as well as to address a headquarters - plant disagreement.

◆ ◆ ◆

C. Random observation

Select random times for the observer to start rounds, in order to see all conditions throughout a time frame, because some work occurs differently at startup, or shift change. Some work occurs during steady state operation and some at changeover. An observer may also stay in the area constantly, finish a round then start another.

Select random paths into, through, and out of the area if at all possible. If the work area is not accessible easily, the observer may achieve a random effect by walking into the area, but not starting observations until reaching a certain point, which may be a column or intersection or simply a good vantage point. Then, look around, make observations, and record.

It is certainly acceptable to stay in the area being observed, and make observations at predetermined times; fill in the time between observations by summarizing data, or other work.

◆ ◆ ◆

D. In advance
The observer must prepare in advance by identifying all of the equipment and people to be observed, and listing all of the categories of activity and non-activity to be recorded.

Let everyone concerned know that you are making a study. When asked, answer questions about your purpose, objectives and technique as accurately as possible.

◆ ◆ ◆

E. Halo effect
The Halo effect, the Westinghouse - Hawthorne effect
"The **Hawthorne effect** is a form of reactivity whereby subjects improve an aspect of their behavior being experimentally measured simply in response to the fact that they are being studied, not in response to any particular experimental manipulation." So says Wikipedia about a set of studies at the Westinghouse Hawthorne work outside Chicago, circa 1924 to 1932, and that is about how I also read today's consensus.

People do react when they are work sampled; you will find that to be common. But they do not all react the same way; some will slow down and some will speed up; in apprehension or just to show you how good they are. (Look for the ones who want to display their talents, because it puts others into a different perspective.) Just be

43

aware that the halo effect exists. Often the people being observed will tire of any unusual effort, in a day or so, and then won't pay any more attention to you.

♦ ♦ ♦

F. Statistics

Accuracy of the study is directly related to the number of observations. An observation is one person or machine, performing one element of work or delay. A major advantage of sampling is that multiple people and machines are observed sequentially, so that the number of observations, and the overall accuracy, increases rapidly.

If the study objective is to quantify "delay", or "work" in total for a group then accurate results will be quickly evident. If the objective is to differentiate between different work elements and different causes for delay during different times of day then the observation sheet will be more complicated and accurate results will take much longer (but probably be more useful).

There are statistical references available that this article does not explore. For work samples, a very useful statistical tool is called a nomograph, on which the number of samples necessary to reach a given accuracy can be determined. Statistical formulae relate the number of observations and the accuracy of results.

If there is statistical expertise available in the operation, you may choose to avail yourself of it. A good rule of thumb is to plot the data and observer the to-date averages. If they settle down, and don't move significantly after a day's data are included, perhaps there are enough observations. If there are significant movements of the running average after entering a day's data, better keep the study going.

♦ ♦ ♦

G. Sampling observation sheet

Use care to set up the sampling observation sheet depending on the objectives. Set it up to collect the information you want and that management desires; be sure to list all pertinent people and processes. And in the study, learn as much as possible to identify problems, to shed light on why they happen, and learn what is required to correct them and get the operation up again.

a) define down time as to material handling, mechanical breakdown, no material, change-over, etc.

b) operator is idle, or absent, at lunch or break, or busy at a particular function

c) operator works alone, or with another. Include all assigned work elements, and be aware that some operators will perform work while being studied that is not their assignment.

d) if the machine is being worked on during delay, record who is there or not there, what are they doing, how long until production resumes. (You may want to shift to a time study of an interruption, to determine exactly what happens and why.)

♦ ♦ ♦

H. Away from the workstation

There will be instances when you do not see a person at the workplace whom you would record. This is a key factor, and deserves special attention to get the right answer.

If you know that the group is at lunch or breaks, you may safely mark that as the activity. (Later on you can cross check the study accuracy by comparing observed and actual "break or lunch".)

If the person has productive work to do only at the work station, and is not at break or lunch, mark the activity as "away". Some away is allowed of course; rest room breaks. Determine whether or not the "away" is excessive by its final percentage of time.

Note generally how conditions are, especially if there are interruptions to work during the study. Enter comments from those involved, because the study objective is to observe "normal" conditions, and if this is an "abnormal" be sure to record that. In a day or so, go to production records and enter on the study what actual output was, recorded lost times, quality issues, rework, etc. Judge then if the study was for "normal" conditions.

If the person has assignments that take place other than at the work station, such as a stockhandler does, record that as away unless you see the person elsewhere and then record the activity observed. When the "away" observations are totaled later, they will not have much significance for this person because you won't be sure just how that time was spent.

♦ ♦ ♦

I. On the floor
So, grab your clipboard with a blank observation sheet, and out you go.

Walk among the person or persons being studied, so that you can observe all the action.

Understand the actions being performed, and their "sequence". If there is something you don't understand, ask. Do not assume.

At the next random time, look around and mentally record the activity of several people, then record on the observation sheet what you saw. When you have seen all you can from that point, move further to see more activity. Record, move on until the circuit is complete. Did you miss anyone? See the section "away from the workstation" and decide how you will record the person's activity. Check the next random time, and get ready for that circuit.

Asking or answering questions does not interfere with the statistical results of the study, as you will not make observations while you talk and discuss.

Act professionally while in the workplace. Use appropriate safety equipment.

Keep your eyes open for problems not on your worksheet, bottlenecks, idleness, safety issues, work stoppage, lack of communication about issues, etc. Make notes first, ask questions later.

◆ ◆ ◆

J. Summary of Observations
All summaries are different. Add the totals, and see what they say, by individual and by group. What are workloads? Are they even among people, balanced through the day? How is time spent? Where is more detail needed? What is a surprise? Where are problems? How did observed activity relate to production records? Make the most of notes on the study.

Good luck, and keep your eyes open.

◆ ◆ ◆

Chapter 5.
Employee Incentive Pay

Or, Piece Work, Piece rate, Work Incentive, Incentive Program, Incentive Plan, Pay for Performance.

The purpose of piece rates is to motivate employee performance in return for a monetary reward.

A simple, valid concept which is centuries old. The purpose of this chapter is to explain the benefits and the potential pitfalls.

An incentive system can be anything a company chooses to make it; tailored for any segment of the work force, designed to reward any kind of performance in any way. While incentives are not necessarily for every situation, in some cases they are a superior strategy. This chapter guides you to understand how incentives might apply to your situation

Some believe that incentives or piecework plans will allow a company to pay less than minimum wage. That is not so. Period.

The sections for this chapter are,
A. Characteristics of incentives or piecework
B. Financial aspects, payback, minimum wage.
C. Where can incentives apply?
D. The special case of construction piece rates
E. Actions to gain many of the benefits of incentives, more simply

A. Characteristics of incentives or piecework

1. Incentives can be effective in any organization.
If you consider incentive pay in a manufacturing setting, that was the original use for incentives and still is as appropriate as ever. But service organizations, and construction firms, and warehouses, and labs and call centers are also prime candidates for incentives. Incentives are quite effective for an individual, a team, or a group.

Incentive plans also include sales incentives and management bonus; the author is not adequately experienced to address these specialties.

2. Why do incentives work to everyone's benefit?
From my experience, incentives are effective employee motivators because most people go to work for money in the first place, and incentives offer an opportunity for them to increase their pay by their own efforts both physical and mental.

But incentives also benefit a company, who perhaps for the first time will measure labor performance and relate it not only to costs but also to output, and calendar performance, and customer service, and capacity.

Wikipedia has it right when they say "An advantage for the company is that this method of payment helps to guarantee the costs per unit produced, which is useful for planning and forecasting purposes."

Good company performance will also motivate employees indirectly because people want to feel that their contribution matters.

3. What employee actions are encouraged by incentives?
Incentives often reward output, or units produced. But any criteria may be selected, such as widgets built or installed, or customer satisfaction, or first time quality, or phone calls, or customers served, or tests processed, or concrete block laid, or applications processed, or feet of cable wired, or cubic yards of concrete poured, or service calls made, or cartons shipped, or tests completed.

The key is to create a measurement system to meet the client's objectives. Usually those objectives are to create a win - win situation, where employees are compensated for actions that benefit employer performance and financial results.

4. Incentives need attention; constant, careful and exceedingly fair
And honest, frank, transparent, timely application, follow-up and judgment.

a. Clear lines of responsibility, prioritized
Define, talk about, write down the specific responsibility and priority that a person has in advance and continually.

b. Measurable performance
An employee should be able to measure his standing, how he is doing. (I know this applies to women and men equally, please allow me to substitute his for his / hers.) This injunction is true for factory or office or field workers; people should and soon will learn how to understand the arithmetic that affects their pay.

c. Ability to affect results
An employee must be able to affect results in order to be held responsible; that statement seems too obvious for inclusion. Watch carefully the measurements applied, and how they are constituted, to understand the ability of an employee to control.

d. Outside the lines
Employees who work with other departments or facilities are difficult to measure directly. Even if their project work has a measureable result, was it because of or despite them? Create another unit of measure to incent those persons with multiple responsibilities.

e. Accurate recordkeeping
Recordkeeping is another obvious requirement of an objective appraisal. Collect the data carefully.

f. Timing
Make appraisals as an umpire does, be on top of the action and call it fast.

g. Change
Organizations constantly change, so features of their work change as well. Incentives affect pay and company cost, be sure to make the investment to maintain the system so that it is fair and correct.

h. How to start: A cost – benefit study
A first step is to define the performance objectives that are important to your company. Then identify specifically what employee actions will help to accomplish those actions; define motivating factors likely to be effective with your work force, and estimate costs and benefits of specific incentive options.

If the preliminary analysis seems to be favorable, the next step is to determine what criteria to use to measure the work that generates the expected output, what reporting and administrative detail would be needed, and the checks and balances to regulate the plan.

i. To put a plan into action
When management decides that a course of action is promising, quickly form the detail to support an incentive plan, define guidelines, determine the expected individual or crew performance

levels, and set up reporting and administrative framework.

♦ ♦ ♦

B. Financial aspects, payback, minimum wage.

1. A key factor to recognize is that workers on piece rates must still be paid at least the minimum wage, state or Federal; and that all work hours must be considered in the minimum wage calculation.

2. Piece rates may, probably will, require more careful reporting

To insure compliance to wage laws, reporting must record not only the production on which piecework is applied but also timekeeping of all hours, and the arithmetic to assure that the letter of the law is followed.

Piece rates involve bookkeeping and labor law in addition to the expectations themselves. The company lawyer and CPA must play a significant part in any actions.

3. Will incentives pay for themselves?

Let's look at the basic premise, which is that productivity and output tend to increase with incentives. Is that written in stone somewhere? Not that I know of.

The benefits for incentives for your organization will be unique. I can't speak to the organization's culture, the local community, or motivation factors.

I do believe that productivity and output tend to increase with incentives. I do believe that, generally speaking, workers will work harder to earn incentive pay. But we also tend to work smarter for more pay, and we will do that before we work harder. Therefore, you had better make all the smart moves before putting up an incentive.

If the following factors are present, perhaps incentives would be successful in your situation.

- ♦ The work to be done is well defined and consistent; materials are available; tools and equipment are maintained; quality standards are well understood and enforced.
- ♦ Scheduling and reporting are reliable; payroll is administered correctly.
- ♦ Delay and lost time are quite low.
- ♦ Waste has been already been removed from the process.

If these factors are not present, I do not recommend incentives. As a matter of fact, management will be quite dissatisfied with incentives, as employees will make the improvements that have been overlooked, and collect an incentive because of it, by working smarter and not necessarily harder.

Instead, your actions should be to correct the inefficiencies first, then judge whether incentives are needed at all.

In any event, balance expected improvement against any extra costs you anticipate.

4. Options to gain many of the benefits with somewhat less structure.

Look again at the points in 3. above. Correct any weak elements in the operation. Especially pull out delay, non-value added activity.

5. If you decide to go ahead with a plan; how should it be structured?

A piece rate agreement is what you make it.

Piece work is nothing more than an agreement, where one party offers what he is willing to pay and another agrees or not.

The typical piece rate in a factory may depend on work measurement, my specialty, but that is not necessarily true elsewhere. There are piece rates for many trades and businesses. These may be time studied, or negotiated, or set near the price that applies locally for the work. In Texas there are piece rates for agricultural workers picking commodities; rates are set by a state commissioner.

So it is certainly practical for you to set piece rates. Set a goal, and pay according to results. I'll be happy to help you set the goals and the reporting mechanisms, but also please see a labor law attorney and your CPA.

In some applications such as apparel piecework plans, the rate paid is essentially all of the labor cost, agreed in advance with employee and buyer, so bookkeeping is simplified and more predictable.

In construction, incentive pay can be tied to the prevailing price paid by local contractors, for instance a value per block laid or square foot of slab, so that estimating and actual cost are more closely related.

Incidentally, a tradesman is typically responsible for quality, so rework would be performed "on the clock". Be sure that quality standards are well defined and enforcement quick and fair. In such cases the minimum wage may apply, so your time system has to be accurate.

Incentives often reward output, or units produced. But any criteria may be selected, such as widgets built or installed, or customer satisfaction, or first time quality, or phone calls, or tests processed, or block laid, or applications processed, or feet of cable, or cubic yards of concrete poured, or cartons shipped, or tests completed. The key is to create a measurement system to meet business objectives.

6. Units

What is measured, what is paid for, can vary according to the organization and product. Generally speaking, use the normal nomenclature, bill of material, router to select what work or output is to be measured.

Assume an operation where widgets are put together, and gizmos are put together, then widgets and gizmos are combined into assemblies. There would be different payoffs for the operators who make widgets, for those who make gizmos, and for those who produce assemblies. The widget line supervisor could be incented for performance of the assigned operators, as could the gizmo and assemble line supervisors. The department manager could be incented for cost and schedule performance of all products, as well as for quality levels. Maintenance could be incented for low downtime.

7. Work measurement mechanisms to collect information

If you measure the work to set an incentive rate, time study and predetermined times are both acceptable mechanisms to collect the information necessary. Work sampling may supplement either, but will not alone be accurate enough to serve as a foundation.

When pay depends on an incentive system, use more care in setting those rates than for measurement which does not determine pay.

If tasks are short cycle, where an operator has considerable practice opportunity, a predetermined time system will be more accurate. Consider MTM, or Work Factor, Master Standard Data, perhaps MODAPTS.

Not only the measurement system determines the accuracy of data collection; a larger number of observations will be necessary if time study is used than would be necessary for a non-incentive system.

8. A View of the Incentive Context

Aubrey C. Daniels, Ph.D., is founder and CEO of management consulting firm Aubrey Daniels & Associates (ADA). He made these comments, with which I definitely agree, in http://www.entrepreneur.com/humanresources/employeemanag ementcolumnistdavidjavitch/article54952.htmlon September 02, 2002. He says, "To get the most out of any incentive plan, I would advise the following:

a. Let the performers track their performance daily. The payout can be monthly, but feedback should be available daily.

b. Separate incentive pay from regular pay. I would advise issuing separate checks and giving them out on different days.

c. Consider non-cash incentives. These are not confused with ordinary pay and actually have advantages over cash. For further details, you may want to read about this in my book Performance Management: Improving Quality Productivity Through Positive Reinforcement, which is available at www.aubreydaniels.com.

d. Individual incentives are more effective than group incentives. You may add an incentive for group accomplishments, but the plan should differentiate between individual contributions and accomplishments.

e. Make sure that your day-to-day management is positive. No matter how much money you put into rewards, you'll waste both money and time if you use negative reinforcement as your management style. There's no substitute for daily contact with employees--asking how they're doing, asking if you can help with any problems and, most importantly, recognizing even small improvements.

f. Systematically evaluate the effectiveness of your plan on performance, cost and employee satisfaction."

◆ ◆ ◆

C. Where can incentives or piece rates apply?
Anywhere the work content can be predicted.
Incentives have traditionally been practiced in a factory setting; piece work has often applied to apparel manufacturing. But other labor intensive activity is also well suited for piecework, for instance:

Construction
- Masonry, block, brick, slabs, beams.
- Dry wall and sheeting installation.
- Piping and plumbing.
- Carpentry. Flooring.
- Energy installation; windmills, solar panels; both commercial and private.
- Electrical, HVAC installation.
- Stucco application, painting.
- Septic tank installation; pumping.
- Roofing.

Agriculture, plant; cultivate; harvest pick and pack. These rates may be set by the state.
Appliance installation
Harvesting trees in consistent conditions such as tree farms.
Hotel housekeepers, maids
Maintenance with a clear work description such as preventive maintenance.

Piecework is difficult to apply to the activity of repair, trouble shooting, maintenance, and warranty because specific content of the work is much less predictable.

◆ ◆ ◆

D. Construction, delivery, off site and remote locations

Incentives and other options will increase productivity and output.

My web site often receives searches for information about construction piece work. Even assuming that many have as their objective to evade minimum wage laws, there is still a real interest in construction piece rates.

From personal experience, there is also a great deal of potential for productivity in construction and other off-site work, and much of it comes before piece work is considered.

Let's discuss some of these components of productivity. In your circumstances they may generate significant savings inexpensively, and if not they will set a foundation for piece rates.

1. Travel, traffic

Construction, delivery, off-site and remote locations will involve travel. Any discussion of travel in this day and age will focus on GPS, global positioning systems. GPS is very sophisticated today and will get more so. It is inexpensive and many commercial applications exist to allow effective route planning; your company should use it for that purpose at least. Instructions to drivers should include GPS input.

When GPS can recognize rush hour, and road construction delays, and the weather, and accident backups, it will become even more useful but that time is not yet I think; stay tuned.

There is at least one more travel factor to consider, which arose with a masonry client of JPR. We talked about the potential problems of setting rates for travel during the day, and someone would mention the hypothetical day in court when an employee would claim the incentive made him drive too fast and he had an accident and got hurt. I'm an engineer and not a lawyer, so I don't know the answer to that nor if that is different from any on-the-job exposure.

2. To improve output, observe the work and correct the problems you see; then improve field reporting.

These actions are very effective and pretty simple to accomplish. Once you have performed them, you may decide you don't need piece rates.

a. Observe

Field and remote operations are commonly less well organized and supported than they are in a central facility; they are less visible and more subject to outside influence. But work measurement (someone with a watch and a note pad is all it takes) can nevertheless define and quantify the circumstances accurately, and lead to better controls. Even without piece rates.

I have often performed time studies in labor-intensive construction sites, and uncovered many inefficient practices which were eminently correctable, and management acted on the problems. Typically,

1. Lost time was prevalent, and study told how much and why it occurred.

2. Crews were too large, often waiting on one another.

3. Correctable constraints were common, usually because some activity was not performed when crews were ready to perform the next operation.

4. The work pace was not what management expected.

5. Travel during the work day was excessive and large crew sizes compounded the loss.

Management, when it learns of these problems, can improve communications, change internal practices and supervision, balance crews, and add equipment based on the results. Then of course after the person with the watch has observed the work, it is easy to establish formal rates and expectations for individuals and crews.

b. Report field results, then read and summarize reports, then act accordingly. A manager can't be everywhere, especially in construction or service. Develop an informative reporting system for the key results, read the information, and let employees know that you monitor activity.

 3. A good sequence, in theory and perhaps for your company, could be:

a. Observe work first; find, judge, and prioritize problems; correct them. See the detail above.

b. Set up reporting forms for high priority / high frequency activities, itemized to isolate actual results. The objective is to determine the actual minutes taken to perform each particular task, over enough jobs to establish a repeatable reliable average. (Note that this time is what occurs, not necessarily how long the job should require.)

Print a series of forms, one for each major task that a crew is assigned. Require crews to complete a form for each project assigned, and each customer. Not only will this report define what people do and how long it takes, it will give insights as to the profitability of each customer, and of each kind of service the company performs. Later feed this information to estimating, or even have estimating receive the information from the field in the first place, and summarize it.

Report travel on specialized forms as well.

Provide columns for start and stop time, name of activity, crew size, quantifying variables such as miles actually driven, time of day, GPS route in miles; yards of earth moved, feet of trench, number of tiles, gallons pumped, customer discussions. Be sure to allow space for the "Degrees of Difficulty", such as rain, rush hour traffic, wait on whatever, site not ready because of whatever, can't proceed because of whatever, name of person / object causing the delay.

c. Have tradesmen / crews / vehicles report on the forms daily.

d. Keep score, summarize and build history. Ask questions to clarify and sharpen field reporting. Issue results back to the field employees.

e. Build intelligence from reports. Look at averages, judge which elements are out of line, or take too long, based on your own experience or further observation. Consider the degrees of difficulty; what is important and what can be forecast or predicted? Build that into expectations.

f. Relate results to project profitability, and to the rates that are part of the local bid structure for work.

g. Then when all these building blocks are in place, consider if the step of incentives or piece rate is likely to be cost effective.

h. You will note that the steps described are similar to any manager or dispatcher's routine; instruct a tradesman what to do, explain how long it should take, and request a report when done, for the next assignment. That's the way to do it, with the minimum paperwork necessary.

4. Construction piece rate measurements possible
If your decision is to adapt piece rates, construction and off site conditions tend to dictate the main guidelines for incentives; the terminology and practices will drive incentives and not vice-versa.

In construction, incentive pay should be very closely aligned to units that estimators quote, that are in their computer programs. These units will usually reflect the local construction market, and reflect the way that contractors and subs submit bids. Incentives for instance can be tied to the prevailing price paid by local contractors, for instance a value per block laid or square foot of slab or roofing square, so that estimating and actual cost are more closely related.

A plan may measure any variable that is important to management. Since different jobs are usually responsible for different results, it is common for different people to be measured for different output.

Chapter 6.
Other aspects of work measurement

A. Performance
1. Low performance usually has a cause, often failure to follow the method or low practice opportunity. Start a closely monitored program to improve, not remove, the individual.

2. If there are official standards, with or without an incentive, be sure employees know what they are and how they perform individually. An employee should be able to calculate their own performance.

3. Rates should be set so that 100% is the expectation. There is something "magic" about 100%, so don't expect 95% or 87%, but 100%.

◆ ◆ ◆

B. Work measurement is not just for direct labor

Direct and indirect labor alike may be measured in the same manner; machinery and processes.
Does an activity contribute to output, customer service, or cost? Its activity can be measured.

For any category, causes of inefficiency can be quantified and corrected
- Imbalance in work assigned
- Procedures, forms can be improved
- Effort is not consistently applied
- Expectations, not stated and / or not monitored

- Manual work is done, can be electronic
- Variable demand for service, perhaps can be smoothed
- Imposed, e. g. requirement for regulatory reports
- Work determined to be unnecessary

Some jobs are repetitive and easily timed; just determine the sequence and record how the times to follow it. Non-repetitive jobs can also be time studied, even if the sequence varies considerably; think maintenance operation or order picker or customer service. The time study form then is essentially a blank sheet of paper. Observe, write down what happens, count the units, record the end of the action, observe the next action. You will need to write adequate notes so that later in the office you can reconstruct and summarize the action. With non-repetitive jobs there is often an opportunity for more than one person to contribute, even an entire crew, so be sure to record those names and tasks and times to the extent possible.

Not only labor but also machinery, processes, techniques, and constraints may be observed, measured, analyzed and managed. These items are often expensive and vital components, and their operating characteristics are critical. The interface between people and the mechanism can be observed and often improved.

◆ ◆ ◆

C. Accuracy
In any kind of work measurement, more observations will generate better accuracy. This is because work measurement is a statistical technique, in which one takes a sample and extrapolates conclusions.

Short cycle jobs can be studied accurately in a shorter time than long cycle jobs because it takes less calendar time to observe the same number of cycles.

There is a corollary, that long cycle jobs tend to be less repeatable in the first place, because of the relative lack of practice opportunity. Short cycle jobs have plenty of practice opportunity and so tend to form a statistically tighter range than long cycle jobs. A further note is that the more common an element, the fewer observations will be needed to meet a particular accuracy level.

There is an accuracy level that is appropriate for your budget and measurement objectives. Generally a higher accuracy is advised for incentives, but a lower level may be acceptable for measured day work and reasonable expectancies.

For specific formulae, please refer to a time study textbook or statistical tract. You will find that you can chart and plot data that you record, using standard control charts and techniques.

◆ ◆ ◆

D. Practice opportunity; learning curve
Short cycle tasks allow the operator more practice opportunity, and the more practice opportunity an operator has, the more rapidly and accurately an operator can perform. A learning curve flattens out after many repetitions, but it still improves.

After many repetitions of hand and finger motions, an operator may develop "ballistic" motion patterns, which repeat within a very tight range. For such patterns, it is generally accepted that a predetermined time system, MTM or Work Factor, perhaps Modapts, will be a more effective and accurate technique than time study.

◆ ◆ ◆

E. The Halo effect, the Westinghouse - Hawthorne effect
"The Hawthorne effect is a form of reactivity whereby subjects improve an aspect of their behavior being experimentally measured

simply in response to the fact that they are being studied, not in response to any particular experimental manipulation." So says Wikipedia about a set of studies at the Westinghouse Hawthorne work outside Chicago, circa 1924 to 1932; that matched what I have read about today's consensus. At the time, the researchers thought that workers were working more productively with more light. But when light intensity was reduced, productivity went up again.

People do react when they are studied; you will find that to be common. But they do not all react the same way; some will slow down and some will speed up; in apprehension or to show how good they are. Just be aware that the effect exists. Often the people being observed will tire of any unusual effort, and then won't pay any more attention to you.

◆ ◆ ◆

F. Products can be observed, yours or your competitors.
Is the new improved version really improved in operation? Can you claim an advantage over the competition? Does a comparison show up a shortcoming that can be overcome? Work measurement can provide objective data as a first step in an action plan.

Sto Corporation web site refers to a time study report that I submitted to them, which show the time advantage to install their construction product compared to their chief competitor.

◆ ◆ ◆

G. Motivation
My own industrial motivation beliefs reflect three well known sources.

1. Abraham Maslow, in his Hierarchy of Needs theory, explained the five needs as: physiological; safety and security; belongingness and love needs; esteem and reputation needs; the need for self-

actualization. In this day and age we like to think most workers have satisfied the first two needs and so their needs are somewhere in the third, fourth and fifth levels.

However if a worker perceives that his job is threatened, that is a level one issue because his very survival is at stake. Are you motivating a person to keep his job or to perform better? A different motivation will be effective in each case.

2. Frederick Herzberg in the Harvard Business Review, *January-February 1968 wrote One more time: How do you motivate employees?*

He identifies job dissatisfiers as separate from job satisfiers, and rated achievement, recognition, work itself, and responsibility as the most significant satisfiers.

3. James Lincoln founded Lincoln Electric of Cleveland which from the 1930's through at least the 1970's was arguably the most productive company in the world. Lincoln Electric year after year increased productivity, cut costs enterprise wide, increased market share. Thousands of companies asked about their success, and Lincoln was very willing to tell them, but none, zero, copied them. Why? Because Mr. Lincoln had two unshakable principals: 1) No one lost his job at Lincoln Electric because of increased productivity. 2) Everyone (except top management) shared in the profits; bonuses for hourly people regularly exceeded annual pay, and they were well paid to start with. Look at http://www.lincolnelectric.com/corporate/about/history.asp for more information.

So, somewhere in this lies truth. Maybe the boss should just buy coffee and doughnuts, because I have seen that as very motivational.

◆ ◆ ◆

H. Bibliography

As I researched this section, I found that the 2011 list of reference data is in pretty sorry state. Even the Institute of Industrial Engineers lists no books with Work Measurement in the title, even my publisher Amazon has few except for those relating to Lean. The following may then be your best hope for classic titles, and many of these books are long out of print. See your friendly librarian.

The Industrial Engineering Handbook is the classic reference for all industrial engineering topics. It is revised periodically. The Third Edition has an extremely extensive series of articles about work measurement and predetermined time systems. H. B. Maynard Editor in Chief, McGraw Hill, 1971. Library of Congress catalog card number 77-128017.

The fifth edition of *Industrial Engineering Handbook* is out, but I do not know how well it covers work measurement.

Motion and Time Study, sixth edition; Ralph Barnes, John Wiley and Sons, 1968.

Time and Motion Study and Formulas for Wage Incentives; S. M. Lowry, H. B. Maynard,
G. J. Stegmerten, McGraw Hill, 1940

Work Design, Gerald Nadler, Richard D. Irwin Inc., 1963

Methods-Time Measurement, H. B. Maynard, G. J. Stegmerten, McGraw Hill, 1948

Work-Factor Time Standards, Joseph Quick, James Duncan, James Malcom Jr., McGraw Hill, 1962

Chapter 7
A Model Plan to Establish Work Measurement

A model plan to establish work measurement will include many of these factors, more or less in this sequence. The scope, degree of emphasis, the amount of formality, the priority of action will depend on the particular organization, and on the purpose for which work measurement is intended. For instance, if incentives are the main objective, then formality of administration will be more important than if line balance is the main purpose.

A. State objectives
List, and prioritize, the purposes that your organization wishes and expects to achieve. Work measurement is an excellent, objective tool to employ in order to:

Quantify expectations for output
Set staffing levels according to demand
Balance workloads
Isolate, remove unnecessary work elements
Find, relieve and manage constraints
Improve work methods, productivity
Establish pay incentives
Build results into scheduling and forecasting
Create standard labor costs for financial reasons
Measure individually or on a crew or group basis

◆ ◆ ◆

B. Define target group
Such as,

One or more particular departments or sections
Direct, indirect, material handling, clerical
Manual or machine related
People or process / equipment

Constraint, or high cost, area
Where staffing level is questioned

♦ ♦ ♦

C. Select the most effective work measurement technique for the purpose

Time study and predetermined times are both acceptable mechanisms to collect the information necessary for work measurement, even to support an incentive system. Work sampling may supplement either, but probably will not be enough alone to serve as a foundation, and certainly not for incentives.

♦ ♦ ♦

D. Outline approach and timetable

Expected benefits, and therefore budget to implement
Phased approach or concentrated
Amount of resources to be applied, and therefore calendar time
Ongoing or one-time project

♦ ♦ ♦

E. Identify internal resources, not only to measure work but also to administer and maintain the resulting system.

People on the staff who are qualified in work measurement
Of the qualified people, who is able to devote adequate time to measurement
Where in the organization chart the responsibility should lie
Reporting path to top management
Support staff, especially supervisory, IT and clerical who will administer the system

♦ ♦ ♦

F. Select any external resources, for training or performance

     From review of internal people, will they need help? If so,

     Best path is to use outside resources to

          train, or lead, or perform entirely?

          train initially, then perform in-house?

     Any equipment required for study or maintenance?

◆ ◆ ◆

G. Communicate

     Within the organization, up or down

     With people

     With involved groups such as unions

◆ ◆ ◆

H. Initiate first study

     Involve the resources needed, in-house and outside.

     Train, plan specific actions

     Communicate closely with the first people involved

     Perform the first studies, summarize and publish

◆ ◆ ◆

I. Review results

     Feedback, compare results, communicate up and down, mid-course corrections

◆ ◆ ◆

J. Retain data

     Set up data libraries and reference systems

◆ ◆ ◆

K. Follow-on studies

Continue study, more areas, products, detail. Summarize, draw conclusions, set rates, publish. Discuss to find potential problems, clarify, resolve.

◆ ◆ ◆

L. Establish reporting and administrative procedures

Establish how activity is reported
Detail how reports lead to follow-up management action
Assign IT and clerical functions to report and follow-up

◆ ◆ ◆

M. Build results into management procedures

Go through the list of management objectives set initially and structure the mechanisms to use the now-available results and data for those purposes.

◆ ◆ ◆

N. Maintain data and program integrity

Keep libraries in order so that they are correct and accessible.

Continue studies for new products and processes.

Monitor actual practice to for adherence to established methods and techniques, and to suggest better ones.

Chapter 8
Manuals for administration of work measurement plans

The following is a draft manual for an incentive or piecework pay system, which will contain more detail than for non-incentive measurement. For your organization, select the appropriate sections as a guide to a personalized manual.

Manual for Incentive Practice

Contents

A. Cover letter from management, prior to development of incentives

B. Cover letter from management, accompanying a Manual of Incentive Practice

C. Plan elements
1. Eligibility
2. Roll out plan
3. Hourly pay plan
4. Supervision pay plan
5. Support staff pay plan
6. Development and maintenance of rates
7. Calculation detail
8. Management discretionary control

A. Cover letter from management, prior to development of incentives

Subject: Development of pay incentives

To: All employees

The company intends to develop and install a pay incentive system shortly. Company management encourages its workers to achieve a high level of productivity and quality and will reward them when they do so through a formal incentives program.

Incentives benefit both employees and management. Employees will know what performance is expected, and will have the opportunity to earn more as they perform more productively. The company will be able to schedule more accurately and to improve the estimating and job costing procedures. Typically employees who earn incentives will reduce cycle times as they do so, so that product sales to customers increase in the same elapsed time.

The company has asked Jackson Productivity Research Inc. to assist us. They will help us to consider cost reduction beforehand; to improve methods, tools, and workplace layout; reduce delay; improve flow. Then JPR will develop the standards for us to use.

A key factor to recognize is that workers on incentive must still be paid at least the minimum wage, state or Federal; and that all work hours must be considered in the minimum wage calculation. As a result, our reporting must record not only the production on which incentive is applied but also timekeeping for all hours, to assure that the letter of the law is followed.

We will determine exactly who is eligible but expect to include hourly employees, direct supervision, and support people; but not management.
Signed,

B. Cover letter from management, accompanying a Manual for Incentive Practice

Subject: Development of pay incentives

To: All employees

The company has developed the following detail for a pay incentive system. Company management encourages its workers to achieve a high level of productivity and quality and will reward them when they do so through a formal incentives program.

A key factor to recognize is that workers on incentive must still be paid at least the minimum wage, state or Federal; and that all work hours must be considered in the minimum wage calculation. As a result, our reporting must record not only the production on which incentive is applied but also timekeeping for all hours, to assure that the letter of the law is followed.

The program will be rolled out during the next few weeks.

Sections to describe the incentive payment plan:

1. Eligibility
2. Roll out plan
3. Hourly pay plan
4. Supervision pay plan
5. Support staff pay plan
6. Development and maintenance of rates
7. Calculation detail
8. Management discretionary control

Signed,

◆ ◆ ◆

C. Plan elements

1. Eligibility
a. Relation to federal and state minimum wage laws
Workers on incentive must still be paid at least the minimum wage, state or Federal. All work hours must be considered in the minimum wage calculation. As a result, carefully record all hours and production amounts. As the program is administered, we will compare earnings with incentive, and compare them to minimum wage laws, to assure that the letter of the law is followed.

b. Hourly
Hourly employees in the following areas will participate:

c. Direct supervision
Direct supervision will participate:

d. Support staff
Support staff will participate:

e. Management
Management will not participate in the incentive plan.

2. Roll out plan
Timing is expected to be as follows:

3. Hourly pay plan

a. Incentive payment does not change the base pay amount
Incentive payment is completely independent of pay scale. An incentive does not change the established base rate of pay. The incentive percentage is first calculated for the time period, and the pay amount earned is determined by multiplying the percentage times the base rate. Thus, if an employee earns 115% for a

particular number of hours, paid earnings will be the base rate times 115%.

b. Individual rates
Incentive rates may be set for individuals, as work is primarily performed alone, with little dependence on the contribution of others other than material handling.

Position   Expected output, units   Per time

c. Team rates
Incentive rates may be set for teams or groups, as work depends primarily on the interaction of different participants. Successful performance can be achieved by cooperation and assistance, by balancing the workload equitably, by maintaining smooth product flow.

Team or group   Expected output, units   Per time

A reasonable expectancy or rate is also completely independent of pay scale. A fair and motivational approach is to reward everyone covered by an incentive at the same percentage rate; a person's pay for a time period will be their individual base pay rate multiplied by the common calculated performance percentage.

d. Quality standards
Quality standards for work apply to incentive conditions. Hours spent by employees to correct quality issues for which they are responsible will be applied as are other work hours.

e. Treatment of non-standard conditions
Non-standard conditions can include times when there is no material available, when incoming material is at an unacceptable level, when a custom job requires special care, when equipment

performance is abnormal, when working conditions or crew assignments are irregular. In these instances, the normal production rates can be suspended, and base pay rates will apply.

f. Reporting of activity from the workplace; timesheets, batch records, etc.
Workplace reporting will be designed to provide for all the time and output variables of the activity, and especially to assure that all provisions of state and federal pay laws are followed.

g. Reporting of performance back to participants
Summaries of actual performance against expectations will be posted for review on the day following the activity.

h. Timing of incentive payments
Incentive payments will be made at the time of the next normally scheduled paycheck. The pay period may be set to allow time for payroll calculation and administration.

4. Supervisory pay plan
        Supervision can have a significant effect on the performance of their employees. Supervisors typically assign work; form crews and work groups; arrange for materials, tools, equipment; schedule; motivate; set priorities; troubleshoot problems; pass on information; report results.

In order to encourage and reward good performance, there is a supervisory aspect to the incentive plan. Supervisors are eligible for incentive pay, based on the performance of the employees under their direct responsibility. Participation by supervisors does not diminish the payment to employees.

a. Basis of incentive pay

The performance of employees over the course of a calendar / pay month (choose one) will determine supervisory incentive pay. A supervisor will be remunerated according to two main factors within the sphere of influence; a) percent achievement while employees work under standard conditions, and 2) as non-standard conditions are minimized.

b. Calculation detail

For the time within the pay period, and for each supervisor:

Determine the weighted average incentive percent paid for all employees within the supervisor's jurisdiction. Determine the percent of work hours performed during standard conditions. Multiply the two together, and the result will be the incentive percent that the supervisor earns during the period.

Example: 15% average incentive earned during standard working conditions for employees. 67% of time spent during standard working conditions. 15% X 67% = 10%, so the supervisor is paid an incentive for the period of 10% of base pay.

c. Timing of incentive payments

A supervisor will be paid the incentive amount at the time of the first paycheck following the completion of the month for which the incentive applies.

5. Support staff pay plan

  Other support, which are not directly involved in the work of those who earn incentive pay, nevertheless can influence performance by their actions. Such employees may include estimators, material handlers, schedulers and planners, clerks, maintenance people; QC, QA, and lab people, those who interact with vendors and clients... Specifically ineligible are those who establish expected performance values, the rates.

a. Basis of incentive pay

The performance of supervisors reflects overall performance during the course of a calendar / pay month (choose one) and will determine support incentive pay. Again, incentive will be a result of high percent achievement while employees work under standard conditions, and 2) low hours of non-standard conditions.

b. Calculation detail

Average the incentive pay for supervisors for a month, and pay support people
1. The same percentage of base pay, or
2. A common factor times the same percentage of base pay, or
3. A pre-determined factor times the same percentage of base pay

c. Timing of incentive payments

Support people will be paid the incentive amount at the time of the first paycheck following the completion of the month for which the incentive applies.

6. Development and maintenance of incentive rates

"Reasonable expectancy"

A "reasonable expectancy" is the output an average experienced employee can routinely produce by applying good skill, effort and pace; using standard methods and equipment.

A reasonable expectancy, an RE, will include all necessary operational work, and the time to set up, clean up, and maintain safe working conditions in accordance with company policy. Rates will include cyclical time and non-cyclical times at the frequency at which they occur, and standard company allowances for break, lunch, and personal time.

RE's will not include any delay time for occurrences within or outside of control of employees or supervision. The elapsed times for delay events will be observed and recorded, and will be administered independently from RE's. The reason for separate administration is that delay times are likely to vary much more than work times, perhaps on a job by job basis, and should not be averaged into RE's.

Reasonable expectancies may be established by normal work measurement techniques, by past performance history, by formal techniques of estimators or combination of measures. An RE will be based on the methods, layouts, crewing, materials and quantities, product and quality specs, and controls which apply at the time; a change in these parameters may result in a change to the RE.

100% performance to a reasonable expectancy should be regularly attained by average experienced tradesmen working with good skill and effort. More than 100% can be achieved by persons who exhibit superior skill and / or effort and / or motivation.

7. Calculation detail

All elements of an incentive plan should be completely open and transparent, all RE's, factors and participation stated, calculations done and results published speedily. A participant should be able to calculate the percentage results themselves.

Typically the process for hourly employees will follow the following routine:

1. Employees report, daily, their production output and type, hours, delay, and other pertinent information.

2. A system administrator will enter the reported information into the mechanism for calculation, manual, electronic spreadsheet, electronic program, or subcontracted service.

3. Instances will occur where more information is required; the administrator will reconcile these.

4. The administrator will calculate performance, in terms of percentage against expected, and will post the results for participants to view.

5. Participants should calculate their own performance, and ask about any perceived discrepancy.

6. Daily results will be accumulated into weekly and pay period summaries.

7. The administrator will compare incentive earnings to minimum wage pay, and set payroll accordingly. A summary of these calculations for each employee will be maintained, on paper and / or electronically to meet appropriate laws.

8. Paychecks will be issued according to company policy.

9. Management discretionary control

The company reserves the right to modify the incentive plan. The objective is to make it as fair as possible, and to motivate employees to take action to reduce project costs while producing a quality product.

It is possible that not all personnel will have an equal opportunity to earn incentives in any given month, but over time opportunity should tend to even out.

◆ ◆ ◆

Chapter 9
Methods and workplace checklists for improvement

Many checklists abound; Frank Gilbreth is a good place to start.

A. The Principles of Motion Economy

In the summer of 1885 a young New England man named Frank Gilbreth began to learn the profession of construction engineer by going to work between two skilled bricklayers. They were to teach him how to lay brick, which was then the basis for most construction.

The men willingly taught him--but they taught him two different methods. Wanting to know which of these methods was best, he quietly stationed himself between two other bricklayers. He found that each of these two men had his own method, and that each method was different from those of the first two men.

Puzzled, Gilbreth went back to work with the first two bricklayers. Careful observation of these men showed that each one used three different methods--one method for working slowly, one method for working rapidly, and the method which they taught him. Gilbreth reasoned that there must be one best way for laying brick, a way that would be both accurate and most rapid.

From this reasoning Gilbreth began a life-long career of studying the motions used in doing many different specific tasks. His unusual abilities as an observer, his great enthusiasm, and his intelligence led him to make many improvements which established him as a successful contractor and later made him known as the father of motion study. Gilbreth's search for the one best way and his systematic approach to motion study also caused him to develop a series of general rules which could serve as a guide in improving most jobs. These he called "Rules for Motion Economy and Efficiency."

Use of the Human Body

1. The two hands should begin as well as complete their motions at the same time.

2. The two hands should not be idle at the same time except during rest periods.

3. Motions of the arms should be made in opposite and symmetrical directions and should be made simultaneously.

4. Hand motions should be confined to the lowest classification with which it is possible to perform the work satisfactorily.

5. Momentum should be employed to assist the worker wherever possible, and it should be reduced to a minimum if it must be overcome by muscular effort.

6. Smooth continuous motions of the hands are preferable to zigzag motions or straight-line motions involving sudden and sharp changes in direction.

7. Ballistic movements are faster, easier, and more accurate than restricted (fixation) or "controlled" movements.

8. Rhythm is essential to the smooth and automatic performance of an operation, and the work should be arranged to permit easy and natural rhythm wherever possible.

Arrangement of the Work Place

9. There should be definite and fixed place for all tools and materials.

10. Tools, materials, and controls should be located close in and directly in front of the operator.

11. Gravity feed bins and containers should be used to deliver material close to the point of use.

12. Drop deliveries should be used wherever possible.

13. Materials and tools should be located to permit the best sequence of motions.

14. Provisions should be made for adequate conditions for seeing. Good illumination is the first requirement for satisfactory visual perception.

15. The height of the work place and the chair should preferably be arranged so that alternate sitting and standing at work are easily possible.

16. A chair of the type and height to permit good posture should be provided for every worker.

Design of Tools and Equipment

17. The hands should be relieved of all work that can be done more advantageously by a jig, a fixture, or a foot-operated device.

18. Two or more tools should be combined wherever possible.

19. Tools and materials should be pre-positioned whenever possible.

20. Where each finger performs some specific movement, such as in typewriting, the load should be distributed in accordance with the inherent capacities of the fingers.

21. Handles such as those used on cranks and large screwdrivers should be designed to permit as much of the surface of the hand to come in contact with the handle as possible. This is particularly true when considerable force is exerted in using the handle. For light assembly work the screwdriver handle should be so shaped that it is smaller at the bottom than at the top.

22. Levers, crossbars, and hand wheels should be located in such positions that the operator can manipulate them with the least change in body position and with the greatest mechanical advantage.

♦ ♦ ♦

B. Consider these principles of motion economy on all jobs

1 Are all motions simple with fewest number of body *members* used?

2. Are both hands free at all times to do useful work?

3 Are the hands being relieved of all work that can be performed by the feet?

4 Are the motions balanced and move in opposite and symmetrical directions?

5 Are the motions rhythmic and smooth flowing with natural movements of the body?

6 Does the motion path stay within the normal working area?

7 Are all tools and materials within easy reach?

8 *Are* the tools pre-positioned ready to use?

9 Are the materials pre-positioned ready to use?

10 Are the materials and tools located in proper sequence at definite places?

11 Does the material come to the operator by gravity or power?

12 Are small objects slid to position instead of picked up?

13 Is it easy to locate the parts in the fixture?
14   Are all the clamping devices of the quick action type?
15   Are devices used to free the hands of holding?
16   Is an ejector being used to remove the part?
17   Is the part removed by drop delivery?
18   Are foot devices convenient with short distances and stops?
19   Are the parts being pre-positioned for next operation?
20   Are the parts being made in multiples?
21   Is the part made with the minimum amount of material?

◆ ◆ ◆

C. Motion Economy Checklist
1. Does each element begin simultaneously with both hands?
2. Does each element end simultaneously with both hands?
3. Are simultaneous arm motions in opposite and symmetrical direction used?
4. Are hand motions of the lowest classification for satisfactory operations?
5. Does motion path stay within the normal working area?
6. Can sharp changes of direction be avoided by using a continuous curved motion path?
7. Are objects slid instead of being picked up and carried?
8. Are materials and tools located in proper sequence at definite work stations?
9. Are the fewest possible elements used?
10. Is maximum use made of rhythm and automatically?
11. Are foot pedals used to relieve hands where possible?
12. Are vises or fixtures used where possible to relieve hands for other work?
13. Can foot operated ejectors be used to remove finished pieces?
14. Can drop delivery be used?
15. Will bringing work close to point of use by gravity-feed hoppers shorten transport?
16. Can prepositioned tools for quick grasp be used?
17. Can pieces be prepositioned for next operation?

18. Is proper height chair with comfortable seat and back rest provided?

♦ ♦ ♦

D. Job Analysis Checklist
1. Rearrange work place
2. Proper equipment
3. Why job done
4. Best product flow
5. Materials at hand
6. Use cheaper materials.
7. Work assignment organized
8. Best job sequence
9. Training
10. Individual productivity records
11. Amount of walking
12. Both hands employed
13. Duplicate other jobs
14. Work double-checked
15. Can job be combined
16. Foot switches
17. Crew balanced
18. Backlog used
19. Suggestions
20. Supervision nearby
21. Job write-up
22. Does job make sense
23. Proper use of relief crews
24. Effectiveness of' crews
25. Job interruptions
26. Workload fluctuations
27. Amount of clerical work
28. Time spent in meetings
29. Effectiveness of individuals
30. Proper use of space
31. Holding device applicable; jigs, fixtures

32. Proper tools
33. Sub-assemblies
34. Machine paced
35. Shorten make-ready put-away
36. Go - No Go gauges
37. Paper work a problem
38. Calculations required
39. Built in delay
40. Frequent change over
41. Waste Control
42. Scrap salvage
43. Brain storming session
44. Forced waits
45. Is job simple

♦ ♦ ♦

Chapter 10
Glossary; terms, and where to find a longer discussion in earlier pages

Glossary of terms, Work Measurement
These terms apply across all aspects of work measurement. This glossary will summarize the definition of each term and cross reference to any more extensive discussion.

Term	Definition
Allowance	a factor added to compensate for such as lunch, break, fatigue, heat, weight; chapter 3 E.
As necessary	portions of an otherwise repetitive job which are only infrequently repeated; also known as non-cyclic; chapter 3 D.
Balanced line	a group of workers with essentially equal work loads
Benefits of work measurement	the reasons why work measurement can benefit an organization; chapter 1.
Best method	the accepted and approved work pattern to perform a task
Bottleneck	the operation that limits a sequence of events
Clock, watch	a timepiece for work measurement
Constraint	the operation that limits a sequence of events
Continuous time study	observation and timing of work in which the watch runs continuously; chapter 3 D

Crew standard   measurement of the work and performance of a crew working together.

Cycle   time from beginning to end, for instance of the work to complete one piece, of an operator or machine

Element   a discrete portion of a job or a cycle, a step; chapter 3 C.

Expectation   that which an average trained, qualified operator will produce over a certain time period, working at good speed and effort. Chapter 2 B.

Expected performance   that which an average trained, qualified operator will produce over a certain time period, working at good speed and effort. Chapter 3 B

External time, the time for work that must be performed by an operator outside the machine operating cycle; chapter 3 D.

Fatigue the effect on the body resulting from work activity during the day.

Fatigue allowance an amount of time allowed to compensate for fatigue during the shift; chapter 3 E

Group standard measurement of the work and performance of a group working together   crew standard

Halo effect, Hawthorne effect reaction of those being studied, caused by the attention to their activity; chapter 4 E.

Incentive, incentives The concept of payment directly associated with the amount of work done, and the formal system for administering the relationship and payment. Piecerate is an example if incentives. Chapter 5

Individual standard   measurement of the work and performance of an individual operator; chapter 3 C.

Internal time   the time for work that may be performed by an operator during the machine operating cycle; chapter 3 D

Lean   Modern techniques based on the Toyota Production System; to eliminate waste and to respect employees

Learning curve   the improvement in elapsed time as more similar operations are performed

Line balance   to place elements of work with selected operators for the purpose of equalizing workloads

Man machine chart a chart of activity and time to relate the relationships of man and machine, Chapter 11, C.

Method   the sequence of events, or work pattern to perform a task; chapter 3 C.

Motion study   the technique of observing and improving motion patterns and methods. Chapter 9.

Non-cyclic   portions of an otherwise routine job which are only infrequently repeated; chapter 3 D.

Non-repetitive   work which is infrequently repeated during the course of a workday

Normal   regular, routine, every day, average

Normal pace   the rate of an average, trained experienced operator working with good speed and effort

Normal time   time required to perform a task at normal pace

Number of observations required to generate accurate results, chapter 3 C.

Observed time the time used by an operator to perform a task recorded during a time study

Observer   the person performing a time study

Operator   the subject of a time study

Pace rate, pace rating   the term used to judge the work done by an operator in relation to normal pace; ; chapter 3 D

PDA   Personal Digital Assistant, an electronic device which can be programmed to time and record elements of a time study; "smart" cell phone

Practice opportunity   frequent performance as similar operations are performed over time; typically improves output.

Pre-determined times are proprietary systems that have over long observation determined the amount of time required for basic motions; chapter 2 C.

Rate   another word for a standard, or expectation

Reading   a time entry recorded by an observer during a time study

Reasonable expectation output that can reasonably be turned out by an employee not on incentive, working at good speed and effort

Red circle identify a instance during a time study that appears to be non-standard, may or not be allowed.

Repetitive work which is frequently performed during the course of a workday

Random sampling observation and recording of work at random times to represent typical activity. Chapter 4

Sequence order of occurrence, especially steps or elements within work activity; chapter 3 C.

Snapback time study observation and timing of work in which multiple watches are used, one of which is reset to zero after each element; chapter 3 D

Standard, time standard an expectation, developed to quantify an objective amount of work

Standard data a composite library of information developed by time studies and their summaries; chapter 3 E

Standard method the approved authorized sequence of events, or work pattern to perform a task; chapter 3 B.

Standard time (observed time x pace rate) plus allowances

Time study the technique of quantifying expected performance objectively with timed observation; chapter 2 C.

Time study form the paper used to record activity and time

Units of measure   expression of quantification; frequency and dimension used to define a value; chapter 3 C.

Value added   activity that increases the worth, as opposed to waste effort or delay

Work measurement   the category that includes time study, work sampling, predetermined times

Work sampling observation and recording of work at random times to represent typical activity; chapter 4.

Chapter 11
Useful forms and worksheets

Useful forms, at least before I-phones and Androids, included time study observation forms, flow charts, multiple activity charts. These forms, for stopwatch study or work sample, are described here, and published on my web site in 8 1/2 x 11, which you may print for use. See http://jacksonproductivity.com/WMforms.pdf

A. Time Study, four forms
Three forms are illustrated, for different use.
1. Use for repetitive time study, when the same elements repeat every cycle. Record readings, then subtract for the elapsed time.

2. For non- repetitive time study; the form will accommodate less structured observations.

3. For crew work sample; the form accumulates activity and workload information.

4. For time study when common tasks may be done in random order. Record time by tasks to yield the information you seek.

◆ ◆ ◆

B. Flow chart
Flow Charts define five possible activities; operation, work, transport, inspect, delay, store. Note that four of these five possibilities do not add value, so first eliminate the non-value added functions.

Flow charting can provide insights into product flow and processes in an office or warehouse or factory, and also the movement of paper, the assignment of work, a customer interface, a service call.

♦ ♦ ♦

C. Multiple activity charts, two forms show relationship and the timing of work elements or activities done, by different people, people and machines, or hands.

For work that is done in parallel, it is often beneficial to define how tasks relate. Common uses of the multiple activity charts include:

1. Man - machine. Typically the objective will be to keep the machine producing, by arranging operator work internal to the machine cycle rather than external.

Define the regular work elements both machine paced and operator paced, find interference, and arrange work to minimize it. You will want to place as much work as possible ""internal" to the machine cycle, and as little "external" to the cycle as possible, so that the machine controls output with minimum wait for the operator.

At this stage, you will want to consider the most effective relationship of machines and operators. One person for each 2 machines, or 3, or 4? Two people per 3 machines, or 4? Seven people per 13 machines? Machine cycles and operator cycles may be such that interference is common unless you are clever with assignments.

Also specifically decide whether to staff for low labor cost or high output. They are not the same. And low labor cost does not mean low product cost, especially if you can sell more product when you produce it. If labor cost is low and machines are expensive, keep the machines busy by assigning more people. Assign more people if you need more capacity, and if you make a profit on the product.

After you have designed the operation as well as possible, there may still be interference because of mismatch in cycles, or unexpected malfunction or breakdown. If the interference is due to